Matthew DiBenedetti, author of *I Hate Everything.*

adamsmedia
Avon, Massachusetts

Published by Adams Media, a division of F+W Media, Inc.
57 Littlefield Street, Avon, MA 02322. U.S.A.
www.adamsmedia.com

Interior illustrations by Elisabeth Lariviere.

ISBN 10: 1-4405-3359-8
ISBN 13: 978-1-4405-3359-4
eISBN 10: 1-4405-3360-1
eISBN 13: 978-1-4405-3360-0

Printed in the United States of America.

10   9   8   7   6   5   4   3   2   1

Library of Congress Cataloging-in-Publication Data
is available from the publisher.

This book is dedicated to everyone but you.

Introduction

Have you reached that point in your life where everybody around you annoys you? Where anything anyone says aggravates you? Where each and every thing—big or small—anybody does irritates you? Me too.

The good thing is, we're not alone. For all of *those* people in the world, there are plenty of *us* people. The kind of people who are sick and tired of being aggravated and irritated and just can't stand it a moment longer. It's not that we're angry or intolerant; it's that we're annoyed these people are allowed to be so, well, annoying. Thankfully, for all of *us* people, there's *this* book.

It's a way to tell *those* people: "I hate everyone!"

I hate people who start long stories with,
"Long story short . . . ."

I hate bubbly morning people.

I hate people who say, "Good morning,"
but their tone suggests otherwise.

I hate people who smile at me when
I'm driving.

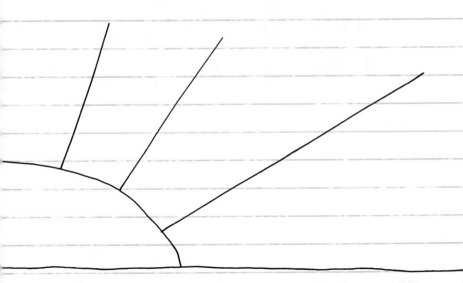

I hate everyone who has those stick-figure-family stickers stuck on the back window of their car.

I hate people who name their car.

I hate people who don't name their private parts.

I hate people who call their private parts by their clinical name.

I hate people who have pet names for their significant other.

I hate people who have figured out their special talent.

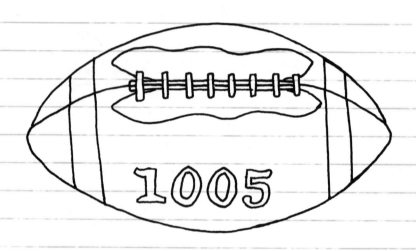

I hate people who enjoy their job.

I hate born athletes.

I hate people who get to play for a living.

I hate young doctors.

I hate young pilots.

I hate people who live over 100.

I hate fortunate people who look younger than they actually are.

I hate dull people who act older than they actually are.

I hate immature people who can't act their age.

I hate everyone who uses an avatar that's better looking than they really are.

I hate studio execs who think all movies
are better in 3-D.

I hate actors and actresses who look better
in 2-D.
I hate writers who make their characters
one-dimensional.

I hate people who don't wipe the ketchup spout clean before closing the cap.

I hate macho men who take over the grill, but have no idea how to barbecue.

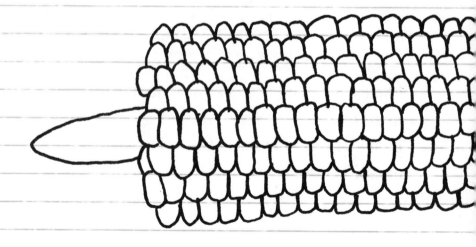

I hate people who don't eat corn on the cob the right way.

I hate clueless picnickers who eat corn on the cob and squirt me in the face.

I hate people who schedule picnics on rainy days.

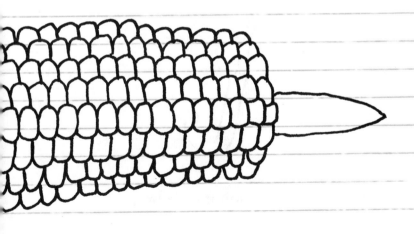

I hate people who hog the umbrella.

I hate anyone who steals the sheets.
I hate people who encroach on MY side of
the bed.
I hate people who have sides of the bed.
I hate people who invade my space.
I hate lovers who have the lost romance.

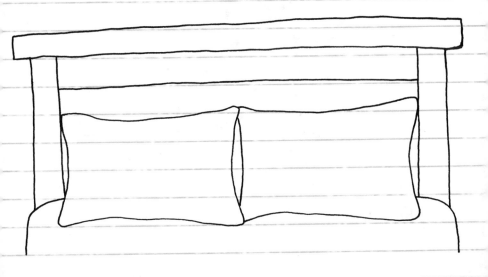

I hate people who play dreadful
songs on jukeboxes.

I hate people who make me listen
to their music.

I hate people who share bad iTunes libraries.

I hate people who won't tell me how much money they make.

I hate people who will.

I hate unfriendly store greeters.
I hate the perky cashier.
I hate fast food attendants who get my
order wrong.

I hate the guy on the phone
who takes my food order,
who I just can't understand.

I hate people who just don't care.

I hate people who order diet soda at McDonald's.

I hate everyone whose diet starts tomorrow.

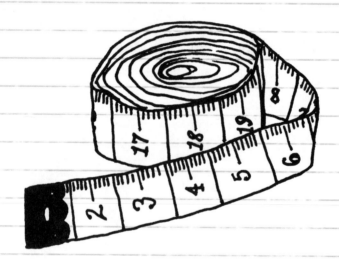

I hate anyone who doesn't have to diet.

I hate the smartass who invented a size zero.

I hate whoever decided male, female, and children's clothing should follow different rules.

I hate any seamstress who has to take my measurements.

I hate anal people who only eat seven chips because that constitutes one serving.

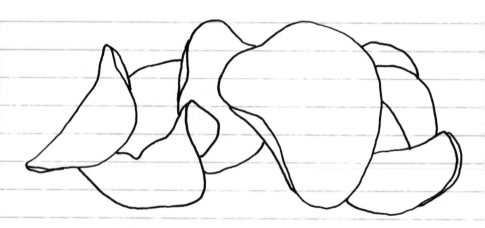

I hate people who go to extremes.

I hate people who get their money's worth
at a buffet.

I hate people who have limits.

I hate people who always are in a good mood.

I hate people who have looked through my boring medicine cabinet.
I hate people at the pharmacy who wonder what's wrong with me when I pick up my prescription.

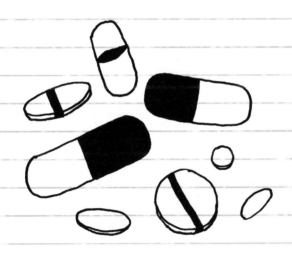

I hate people who don't think they need happy pills.

I hate people who see the glass half full, even when it is half empty.

I hate people who never have anything nice to say.

I hate people who rain on other people's parade.

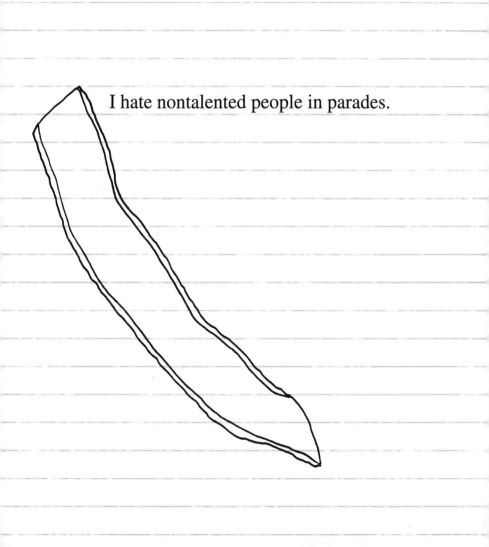

I hate nontalented people in parades.

I hate everyone over the age of twelve and under the age of sixty who wears tighty-whities.

I hate kids over six months who still wear diapers.

I hate older men who wear their pants too high.

I hate anyone who asks, "Boxers or briefs?"

I hate everyone who expects change to happen by itself.

I hate everyone in an opposing political party.

I hate movie presidents who give more historic motivational speeches than real-life presidents.

I hate clever people who throw
better themed parties than me.

I hate anyone who has the day off when
I have to work.
I hate carefree people who can surf every day.
I hate people who order surf with their turf.
I hate people who live in tropical locations.
I hate people who settle.

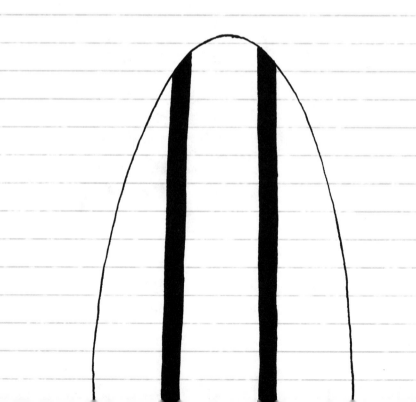

I hate anyone who makes skiing look easy.

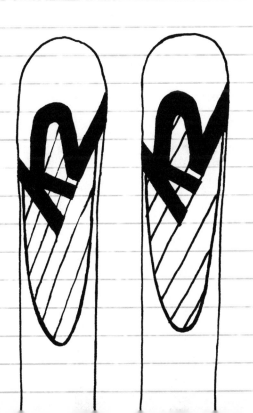

I hate everyone whom corrects my grammar.

I hate people who don't know when to use who or whom.

I hate people who correct you, but are wrong.

I hate soon-to-be unfreinded people who point out my typo's on Facebook.

I hate strangers who try to "friend" me on Facebook.

I hate everyone I've tried to "friend" on Facebook who hasn't accepted me.

I hate people who "unfriend" me without a reason.

I hate everyone who I've "unfriended," but who haven't noticed.

I hate everyone who speaks in txt chat out loud. LOL

I hate people who don't really LOL.

I hate everyone who has actually Laughed their Ass Off.

I hate everyone who has ROTF.

I hate everyone who isn't funny enough to make me ROTFLMAO.

I hate clowns.

I hate everyone who isn't funny enough to make me ROTFLMAO.

I hate clowns.

Your friend is no longer available.

I hate people who sign off while I'm chatting with them.

I hate the "new friends" who I've acquired through my new relationship.

I hate friends who change when they start dating someone new.

I hate people who disappear whenever they get involved in a relationship.

I hate those same people even more when they come back after the relationship ends . . . again.

I hate people who pretend to like you.

I hate inexperienced partners.

I hate partners who have WAY too much experience.

I hate absolutely everyone who my significant other has ever dated.
I hate everyone who my ex dates going forward.

I hate anyone who gives a lousy massage.
I hate people who get massages but don't
reciprocate.
I hate people who ask for a massage,
then say you're doing it wrong.

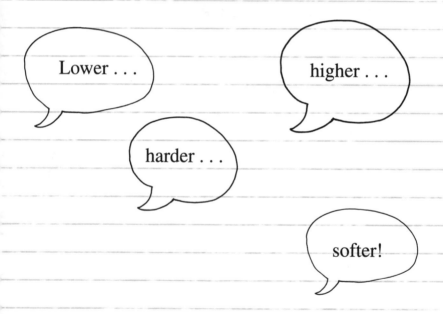

I hate friends who say my mother is hot.

I hate girls who just wanna have fun.

I hate people who don't make more time
for fun.

I hate friends who get together and have fun
without me.

I hate people with babies who always make *you* visit *them*.

I hate parents who don't control their kids in public.

I hate anyone who takes their kids out in public.

I hate people who don't keep their children on a leash.

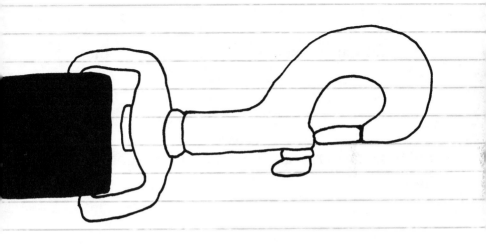

I hate people who think it's okay to bring their dog to my house.

I hate famous rappers who keep changing their name.

I hate gangsta rappers who star in feel-good movies.

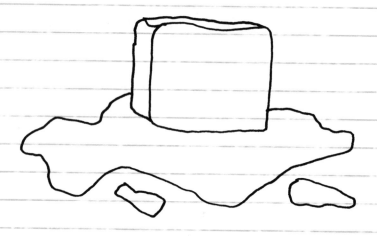

I hate pop stars who sample other songs to help make their song popular.

I hate artists who feel compelled to announce their name in all their songs.

I hate famous people who go by one name.

I hate UN-handy men who work at
Home Depot.
I hate ice cream scoopers who skimp when
filling MY cone.

I hate any waiter who needs to be reminded to
wash their hands after using the bathroom.

I hate cashiers who have to ask for my phone number.

I hate everyone who has ever given me a phony number.

I hate anyone who actually gets a "booty call."

I hate people who text me by mistake.

I hate everyone who has a friend with benefits.

I hate my friends who don't really have any
benefits to share.

I hate people who have found a sugar daddy
or mama.

I hate people who use fake sugar.

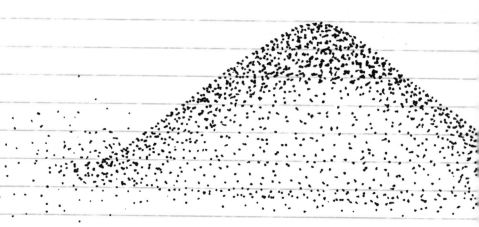

I hate people who mow their lawn at the crack of dawn.

I hate people who can't sleep and feel it's okay to keep you up with them.

I hate people who always have energy.
I hate people who are always tired.
I hate people who make me yawn, by yawning.

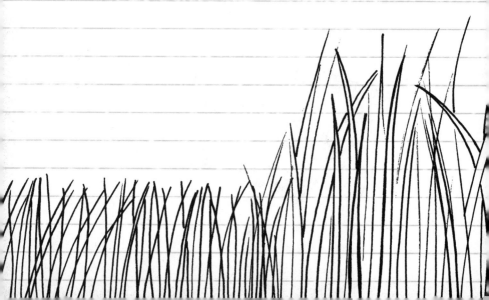

I hate that nobody has shook me all night long.

I hate anyone who doesn't give out candy
on Halloween.
I hate kids who don't say trick or treat.
I hate trick-or-treaters who don't wear
costumes.

I hate those who trick,
but don't treat.

I hate the ghosts who haunt me.

I hate the skeletons in my closet.

I hate people who unload all their skeletons on the first date.

I hate people who wait until it's too late to unload their baggage.

I hate people who are always too busy to
make plans.
I hate people who have people.
I hate people who say, "You'll have to take that
up with my lawyer."
I hate myself for helping make the rich richer.

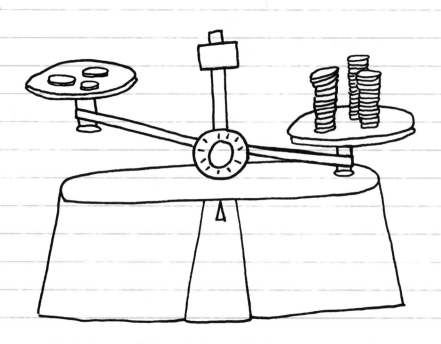

I hate rich people who are dicks.

I hate people with the name Rich that go
by Dick.

I'd hate me if I were rich.

I hate Lady Gaga for not *wanting to be friends*.

I hate people who have a good poker face.

I hate people who say, "Poker? I hardly know her."

I hate people who poke each chocolate in the mixed box to find the filling they like.

I hate coworkers who empty my candy dish when I'm not around.

I hate people who have time to play
solitaire at work.

I hate people who play solitaire
outside of work.

I hate people who are too good
to be true.

I hate anyone who has totally
gagged me with a spoon.

I hate people who try to make up
a hot new saying or catch phrase.

I hate anyone who still wears sweatbands, whether you work out or not.
I hate people who wear baseball caps sideways.
I hate anyone under ninety who wears a visor.
I hate punks who wear their pants off of their asses.
I hate women who are okay with showing their panty lines.
I hate anyone who wears white after Labor Day.

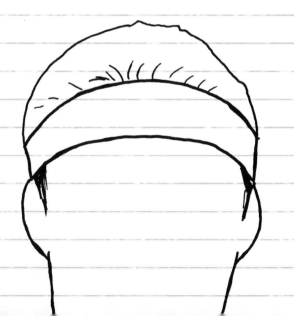

I hate movie critics who hate the movies I love.

I hate people who can stump me with their favorite movie lines.
I hate anyone who doesn't get the movie lines I quote.
I hate scruffy looking nerf-herders.

I hate anyone who thinks Chewbacca was male. She loved Han!

I hate all the characters in *Star Wars* who were on screen for a split second who have an action figure.

I hate anyone who thinks it's impossible to bulls-eye a womp rat in a T-16.

I hate mundane people who don't post anything
of value on Facebook.

I hate people who don't pay attention to me.

I hate people who need a hobby.

I hate people who lack social skills, but live
their lives through social media.

I hate people who collect things.
I hate people who save things thinking they'll
be worth something someday.
I hate people who buy me things because they
think I collect them.
I hate anyone who can sit through those hoarder
reality shows.

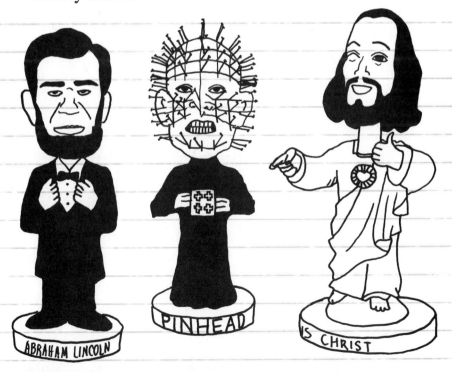

I hate girls' friends who know too much detail
about each other's boyfriends.
I hate anyone who is a bigger person than me.

I hate people who look down at me.
I hate people who give me their overflow
garden veggies.
I hate showoffs.

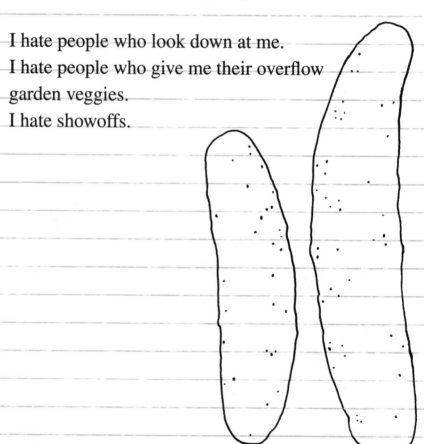

I hate self-proclaimed experts.

I hate people who look the other way when they shouldn't.

I hate anyone who won't bend the rules just this once.

I hate people who stretch before exercising.

I hate people who push the boundaries on corporate attire.

I hate people who take a mile when you give them an inch.

I hate people who have accidentally worn their shirt inside out.

I hate people who need rules.

I hate everyone who thinks they can flip a house.

I hate the Wicked Witch of the West.

I hate the boogey man who lived in my closet while growing up.

I hate people who don't realize they have a booger visible.

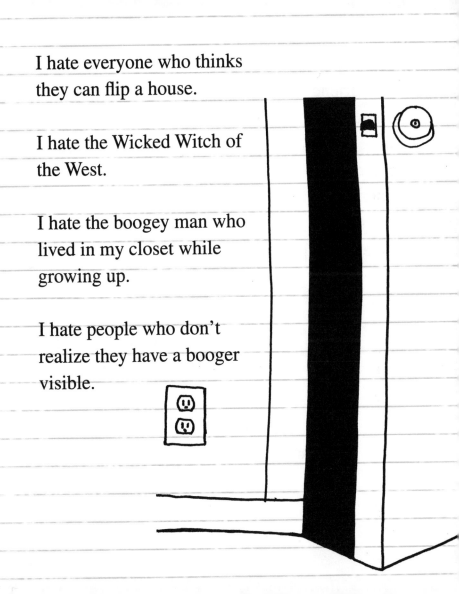

I hate friends for not being real friends when you need them most.

I hate people who keep me around only to kill spiders.

I hate people who only call when they need something.

I hate needy people.

I hate clingy people.

I hate bands who start songs with the innovative
. . . 1 . . . 2 . . . 3 . . . 4!
I hate lead singers who use made up fillers like
nah nah nah.
I hate great bands who break up because they
just can't get along.
I hate musicians who think they can act.
I hate actors who think they can sing.

I hate everyone who CAN dance.

I hate people who think they can dance.

I hate people who know how to dance . . . who dance with my date.

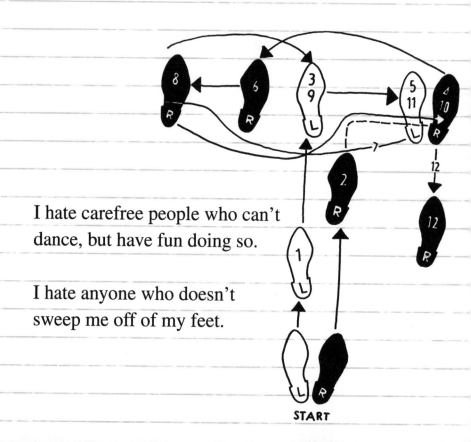

I hate carefree people who can't dance, but have fun doing so.

I hate anyone who doesn't sweep me off of my feet.

I hate people who wear their sunglasses at night.

I hate the guys who are way too old to be in the same nightclub as me.

I hate the visibly sweaty pits dancing guys, who dance up on you.

I hate the unapproachable "thinks she's hotter than hot" chick.

I hate people who remove their wedding ring while out.

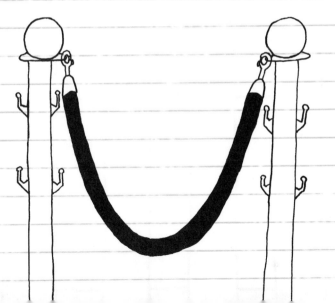

I hate people who openly check out and smile
at my partner . . . while I'm right there!

I hate people who have no boundaries.
I hate leaders who fight over boundaries.
I hate the Joneses.

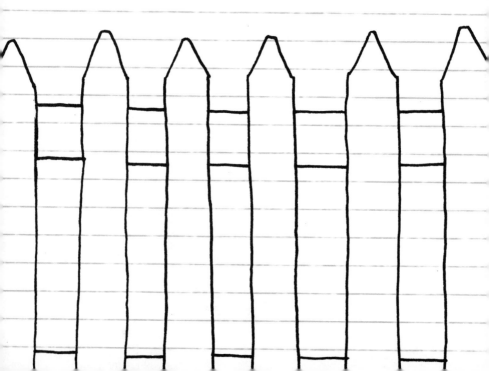

I hate everyone in an entourage.

I hate everyone who wants a free ride.

I hate everyone who becomes your friend when you get a pool.

I hate every attractive person on TV who my partner tells me is HOT.

I hate actors who have only made it on their looks.

I hate people who don't act on their feelings.

I hate people who have had intimate dreams about me, but never told me.

(I'd hate if nobody had intimate dreams about me.)

I hate losers who get lucky.

I hate people who choose plastic over paper when bagging groceries.

I hate store chains who advertise things they don't have in stock.

I hate people who block the one item you want on the shelf with their shopping cart.

I hate everyone who looks at the stuff I'm buying when I'm at the register.

I hate people who eat healthier than me.

I hate the judgmental grocery store cashier who can tell I'm buying food for one.

I hate people who talk on their cell phone while checking out at the register.

I hate the old lady with eighteen items in the ten-item checkout line . . . paying in pennies.

I hate my cast of friends for not wanting to hang out in a coffee shop every day.

I hate TV execs who ruin good TV shows with nonstop syndication.

I hate that single cast member who brings something great to an end. #WINNING

I hate radio DJs who play great songs to death.

I hate iconic stars who could've
prevented their untimely death.

I hate selfish people.

I hate everyone who has copied Justin Bieber's hairstyle.

I hate unoriginal people.

I hate famous people who set trends with their hairstyle . . . that I've had for years.

I hate everyone who has nicer hair than me.

I hate anyone who is ballsy enough to try new hairstyles.

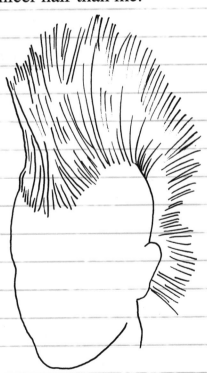

I hate people who tell me that I should try a new hairstyle.

I hate anyone who touches my hair.

I hate people who can get away
with going to the barber.

I hate hairdressers who always
take more off than I've asked.

I hate hairdressers with bad hairstyles.

I hate girls who have long beautiful hair, but only pull it back into a ponytail.

I hate girls old enough to know better, who still wear side ponytails.

I hate little girls who actually got a pony as a gift.

I hate people who brag.

I hate everyone who dresses better than me.
I hate people who always wear the latest
fashion trends.
I hate people who underdress for occasions.
I hate people who can pull off wearing
bold hats.

I hate people who look better in the same clothes I wear.

I hate fitness junkies who don't wipe their sweat off the gym equipment after using it.

I hate people who spend an extra ten minutes on the treadmill so they can eat dessert tonight.

I hate people who have time to exercise.

I hate everyone whose daily goals include: gym, tan, laundry.

I hate everyone who makes more than me for doing less.

I hate everyone who fist
pounds and explodes.
I hate every radio and TV host
who says, "fist pump."

I hate people who try too hard
to be cool.

I hate people who don't buy knock-off name brand purses.

I hate people who flash around their fancy jewelry.

I hate everyone who comes into money through marriage.

I hate everyone who has inherited their money.

I hate my older relatives for not being wealthier.

I hate rich people who haven't
asked to marry me.

I hate people who have roosters as pets.

I hate people who ask, "How are you doing?" but don't really care.

I hate myself for answering them.

I hate everyone who makes me not want to care anymore either.

I hate people who don't have a care in the world.

I hate people who go on and on about themselves.

I hate people who love the sound of their own voice.

I hate everyone who asks me for my opinion.

I hate people who don't take MY "optimistic" advice.

I hate waiters who ask how everything was . . .
before I've taken a bite.
I hate waiters who rush you.
I hate waiters who seem annoyed to be
serving you.

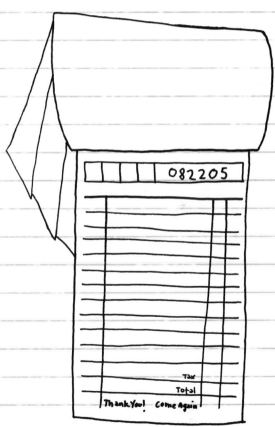

I hate people who don't do their job.

I hate people who rely on you.

I hate unreliable people.

I hate people who are sick and come to work.

I hate anyone who has come down with
Bieber fever.

I hate people who ARE more fun when
they drink.
I hate everyone who is funnier than me.
I hate people who are quick with their wit.
I hate people who do better practical jokes.

I hate anyone who doesn't get my humor.

I hate people who don't feel guilty about sleeping in.
I hate people who make me feel guilty for doing the things I enjoy.

I hate people who do a lot of talking, but not a lot of doing.

I hate people who continually repeat themselves.

I hate people who continually repeat themselves.

I hate people who continually repeat themselves.

I hate people who continually repeat themselves.

I hate people who continually repeat themselves.

I hate people who continually repeat themselves.

I hate people who continually repeat themselves.

I hate people who continually repeat themselves.

I hate people who continually repeat themselves.

I hate people who continually repeat themselves.

I hate people who continually repeat themselves.

I hate people who continually repeat themselves.

I hate people who continually repeat themselves.

I hate people who continually repeat themselves.

I hate people who continually repeat themselves.

I hate people who continually repeat themselves.

I hate people who continually repeat themselves.

I hate people who think the world
revolves around them.

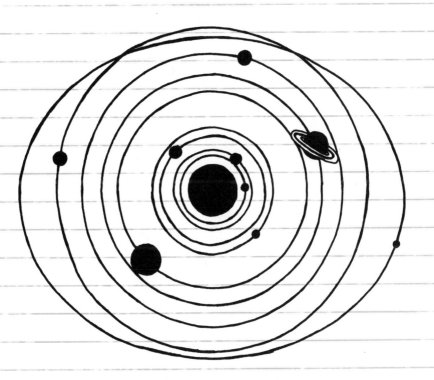

I hate anyone who lives in their
own fantasy world.

I hate ignorant people.
I hate people who hate people for what
they believe.
I hate people who don't make wishes on
shooting stars.
I hate people who don't believe in miracles.
I hate people who don't believe.

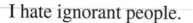

I hate everyone who doesn't do something they want because they're afraid it's not cool.

I hate anyone who has never made a snow angel.

I hate people who care what other people think.
I hate people who don't have an open mind.
I hate people who don't open their wallets.
I hate lobbyists who are in it just for the money.
I hate complainers who don't do anything
about it.

I hate people who don't say hi back.

I hate people who judge me for:
- [ ] the way I look.
- [ ] the car I drive.
- [ ] the clothes I wear.
- [ ] the friends I have.
- [ ] the place I live.

I hate friendly strangers who smile and say hi.

I hate friends who have their own language.

I hate fans who obsess over sports.
I hate sports fanatics who don't play sports.
I hate lame mascots.
I hate team captains who picked me last.
I hate that kid who broke my school record. . . .
(However, I'm somewhat okay with the kid
who broke his.)

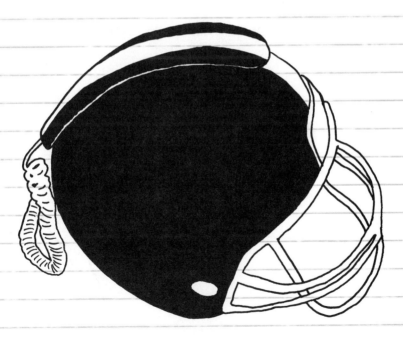

I hate Disney fanatics who
wear Disney everything.

I hate people who own more than one cat.

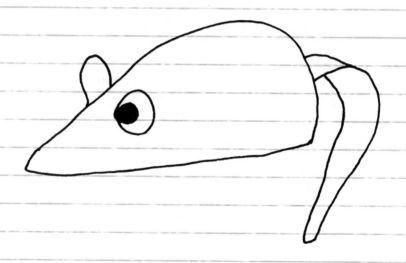

I hate family members who embarrass me by leaving a lousy tip.

I hate friends who don't want to split the bill evenly.

I hate "those" friends who always skimp on their portion of the bill.

I hate those people who complain in
every restaurant.

I hate waiters who don't take revenge.

I hate people with bad pickup lines.
I hate people who reject my flirting.
I hate people who are always cold.

I hate people who are hot.
I hate people who know they are hot.

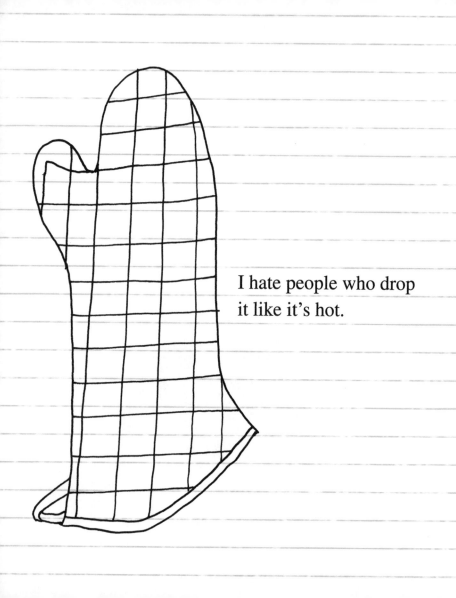

I hate people who drop
it like it's hot.

I hate girls who have planned out their entire wedding . . . but aren't dating anyone.

I hate brides who we all know shouldn't be wearing white.

I hate fiancées who invite their exes to their wedding.

I hate when the best man really isn't the best man.

I hate the insane girls who fight to catch the
bridal bouquet . . . thinking it will help.

I hate bridezillas.

I hate the controlling mothers of bridezillas who must throw the perfect wedding shower to show off.

I hate people who try to upstage the bride.

I hate "family" and "friends" who forget it's not their wedding.

I hate the people I get stuck with at the mish-mosh, leftover wedding guest table.

I hate lousy wedding singers.

I hate people who know every line dance . . .
even the sexy extended versions.

I hate people who leave people at the altar.

I hate people who are always late.

I hate people who go through with getting married . . . but didn't want to.

I hate people with cold feet.

I hate people who don't cuddle.

I hate ex-loves of your life who you end
up hating.

I hate cupid for having lousy aim.

I hate people who are in that stupid puppy love phase.

I hate people who are soooo openly in looove.

I hated my parents during every second of
"the talk."
I hate people who openly talk about their sex
life with their parents.
I hate parents who still have sex.
I hate old people who still talk about
having sex.

I hate couples who fight CONSTANTLY.

I hate people who would rather stay together than be alone.

I hate people who don't leave me alone.

I hate loners.
I hate people who never return what you loan them.
I hate people who cash in on favors.
I hate people who borrow things.
I hate people who say, "Payback's a bitch," . . . and haven't paid me back yet.

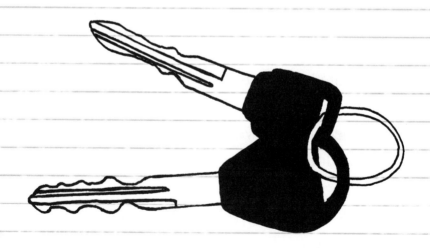

I hate people who critique everything I do.

I hate perfectionists.

I hate people who think they are perfect.

I hate snooty people.
I hate snotty people.
I hate kids with runny noses.

I hate people who won't admit that they liked Episodes I–III.

I hate clones.

I'd hate my clone.

I hate Luke Skywalker for not ruling the galaxy as father and son.

I hate anyone who hasn't seen *Star Wars*.

I hate everyone who confuses *Star Wars* with *Star Trek*.

I hate people who touch my bobblehead.

I hate people who use their outside voice . . . inside.

I hate people who forget what they were talking about.

I hate people who lack focus.

I hate anyone who makes it hard to get ahead.

I hate anyone who has ever ruined a holiday or a vacation.

I hate the person who inspected my pants;
you know who you are, Inspector #23.

I hate people who want to argue.

I hate people who can argue better than me.

I hate people who win.

I hate people who cheat to win.

I hate myself when I lose.

I hate sore losers.

I hate people who play dirty.

I hate people who always have a
one-track dirty mind.

I hate people who eat bananas
in public.

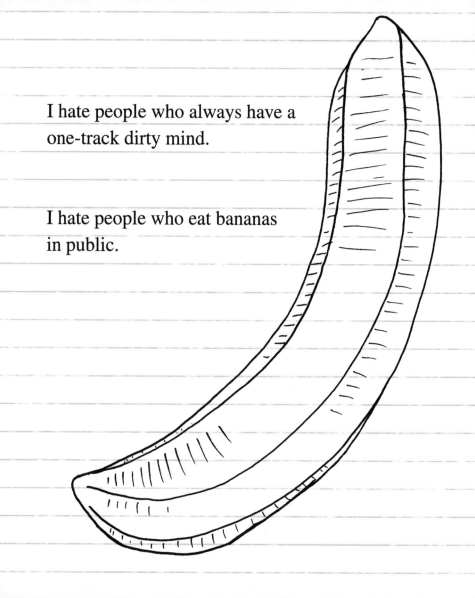

I hate people who have plastic on their furniture.
I hate people who don't live for today.
I hate people who wait for destiny.
I hate people who don't realize what they have right in front of them.
I hate people who don't stop to smell the roses.

I hate people who don't listen
to their own advice.

I hate people who don't realize
they're wasting my time.

I hate everyone who is fine with the status quo.

I hate people who never leave their hometown.

I hate people who have more
than one best friend.

I hate people who claim their
significant other is their best friend . . .
but they don't tell them everything.

I hate hypocrites.

I hate people who hop on bandwagons when
a team is winning.
I hate sports fans who yell at the athletes
on TV when watching sports.

I hate grown men who have cried
in front of other men.

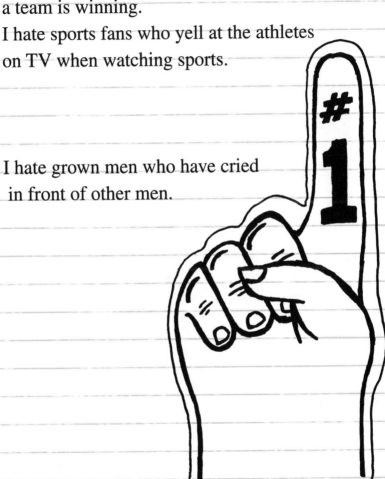

I hate sports stars who get paid
waaaay too much.
I hate superstars who are role
models, who shouldn't be.

I hate people who don't eat unhealthy
food when watching sports.

I hate guys who defend getting manicures.
I hate girls who only date bad boys.

I hate people who don't clean under their nails.
I hate nail manicurists who talk about me in
another language.
I hate people who bite their nails.
I hate people who pile up their nail clippings.
I hate people who save things for a rainy day.

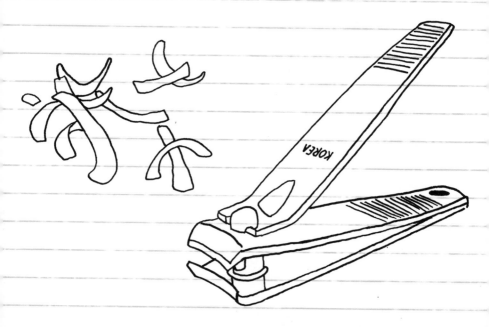

I hate girls who wear makeup at the gym.

I hate girls who don't need makeup
to look good.

I hate the guy who works out so much he can't put his arms down.
I hate people who intimidate me.
I hate that other gym guy who walks around with his arms out who thinks he has big muscles.
I hate mama's boys.

I hate the shirt-unbuttoned-too-low, hairy-chested gold chain guy.

I hate people who are tan during the winter months.

I hate people who touch my back when I'm sunburned.

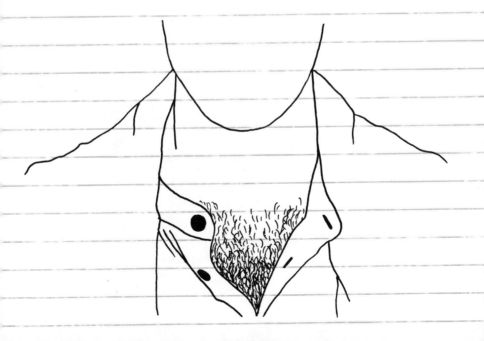

I hate the sixty-year-old, spray-tanned
Speedo bathing suit guy.
I hate everyone who tans more than they
should.
I hate people who don't tan, but should.

I hate people who never realized the benefits
of sunscreen.

I hate class clowns.
I hate the life of the party.
I hate people who can't burp the alphabet.
I hate party poopers.

I hate unfunny comedians.
I hate people who $%&#ing curse too much.
I hate dirty roommates.
I hate people who offer you a warm tissue from their pocket.

I hate corporate leaders who profit from all my hard work.

I hate lazy paperboys.

I hate bosses who yell.

I hate people who have actually had the guts to not take it any more, and quit their job on the spot!

I hate quitters.

I hate people who get promoted because someone left above them.

I hate anyone who is more successful than me.

I hate mimes.

I hate clumsy people.

I hate people who slow down
to look at an accident.

I hate people who cut in line.

I hate drivers who deserve to
get a ticket, but don't.

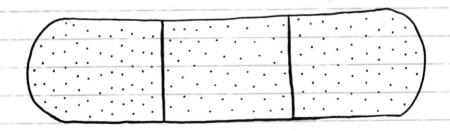

I hate truck drivers who don't blow their horn when you give them the arm pull signal.

I hate drivers who lean on their wimpy foreign car horn and expect me to be intimidated.

I hate people who don't stop for stranded cars.
I hate people who only stop if the stranded
person is attractive.
I hate attractive girls who can talk their way out
of a ticket.

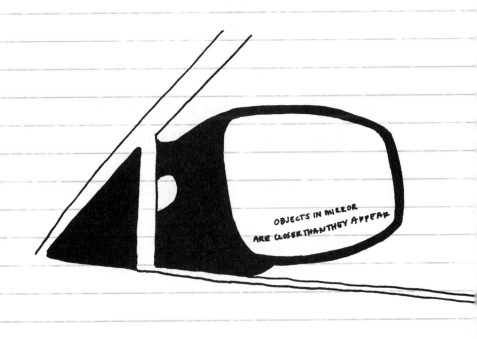

I hate people who request a "read receipt"
on EVERY e-mail they send.

I hate coworkers who claim everything is hot.

I hate people who send viruses
and spam my e-mail.

I hate the people of Troy who were dumb
enough to fall for the Trojan horse.
I hate gladiators who are bigger
and stronger than me.

I'd hate Medusa if I ever saw her.

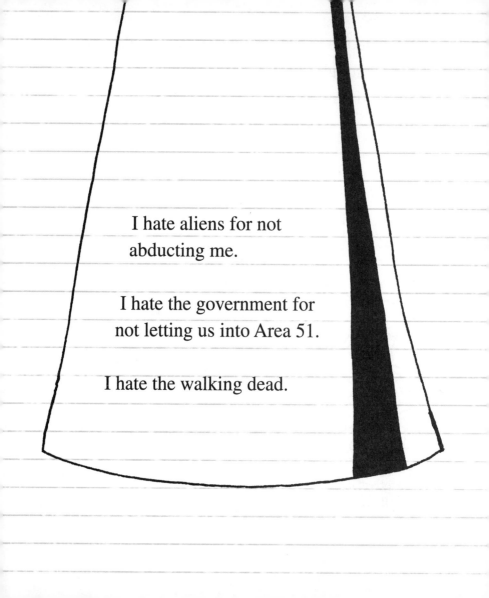

I hate aliens for not abducting me.

I hate the government for not letting us into Area 51.

I hate the walking dead.

I hate everyone who carries their dogs.
I hate people who let their dogs walk them.
I hate big men with little fluffy dogs.
I hate owners who feed their dog table scraps,
then yell at it for begging.

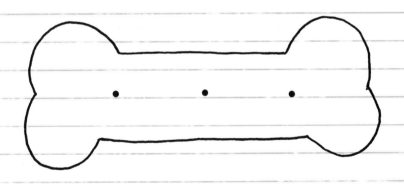

I hate people who say, "atta boy!"
I hate people who call me boss, who don't
work for me.
I hate non–American Indians who call me chief.
I hate non–little people who call me big guy.
I hate people who think they are more
important than you.

I hate people who have called me by the
wrong name.
I hate um, you know—what's his face . . .
and people who can't remember names.

I hate people who grind their teeth
in their sleep.

I hate everyone who I can hear snore.

I hate neighbors.

I hate idiots who park in front of my mailbox.

I hate people who e-mail me
instead of texting me.

I hate people who don't respond to my e-mails.

I hate people who have managed
to stay off the grid.

I hate elves who don't make cookies.
I hate elves who only make wooden toys.
I hate people who don't get with the times.

I hate people who don't listen.

I hate people who eat the ears off
the chocolate bunny first.

I hate people who have toes bigger than their BIG toe.

I hate people with hairy monkey knuckles.

I hate men with puffy-hairy backs.

I hate men who are oblivious about the wild hair-forest growing out of their nose and ears.

I hate numb people who don't realize they have food on their face.

I hate people who want to try your
food when eating out.

I hate people who want to lick from
my ice cream cone.

I hate people who don't share.

I hate people who won't try a sip from
my drink.
I hate people who leave backwash.
I hate people who swim the backstroke.

I hate people who ask me to take their picture, and then don't like it.

I hate "friends" who tag me in pictures online without my approval.

I hate those people who post comments on EVERY Facebook post.

I hate people who Facebook stalk.

I hate people who have realized that I Facebook stalk them.

I hate people who block their photo albums.

I hate Facebook users who "poke."

I hate people who don't want to "poke" me.

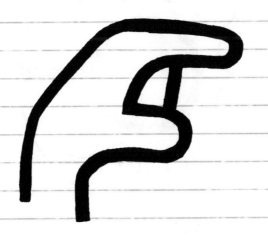

I hate everyone who isn't on Facebook yet.

I hate everyone who is still using MySpace.

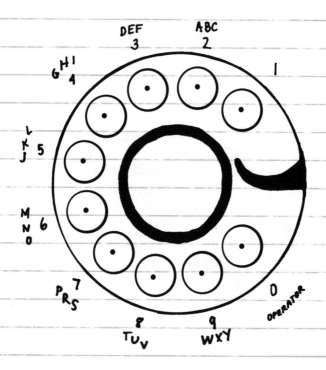

I hate people who think they have the next Facebook.

I hate people who are left behind.

I hate the people at Google who know EVERYTHING about me.

I hate movie villains who have large fish tanks.

I hate villains who reveal their sinister plan just before they are ready to dispatch the guy. I hate people who escape my clutches.

I hate people who will still watch crappy
TV, when nothing is on.
I hate horror movie actors who were just put
there to be brutally murdered.
I hate twentysomethings who play high-
schoolers in TV shows.

I hate teen icons who have perfect teeth.

I hate people with fake smiles.
I hate people who don't smile.
I hate Botox addicts.
I hate people who can't smile.

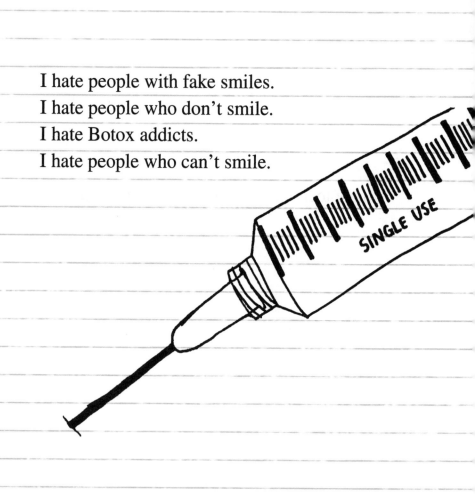

I hate women who claim they didn't get
a boob job.
I hate young people who get "work" done.
I hate people who resemble their pet.

I hate bachelorette parties who coordinate
their clothing.
I hate people who wear tiaras.
I hate people who act like princesses.
I hate spoiled brats.

I hate people who introduce significant
others only by their name.

I hate busted cheaters who try to blame you.

I hate people who tell two lies
to cover up another.

I hate people who begin to
believe their own lies.

I hate people who are only famous because of their parents.

I hate semi-famous people who say, "Don't you know who I am?"

I hate the True Hollywood Story stars that we are left with.

I hate people who look like famous people.

I hate people that we made famous who won't sign autographs.

I hate famous people who have their own
fragrance line.
I hate people who want to smell like famous
people.
I hate actors who stink.

I hate people who talk loudly during flights.

I hate nosy people next to you on the plane who feel obligated to ask about your travels.

I hate the women with the screaming babies who always seem to sit next to me during transcontinental flights.

I hate kids during any form of travel.

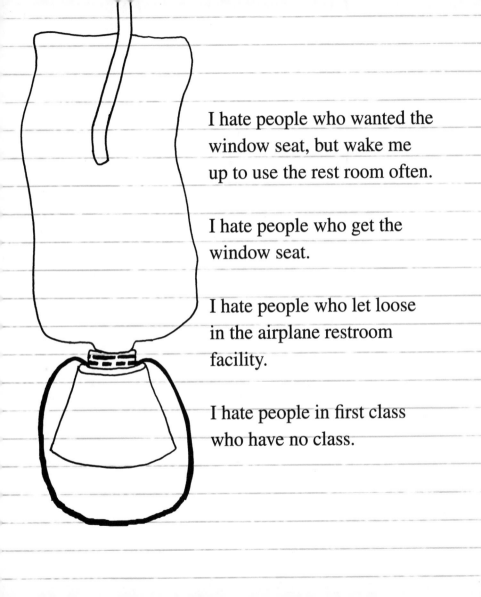

I hate people who wanted the
window seat, but wake me
up to use the rest room often.

I hate people who get the
window seat.

I hate people who let loose
in the airplane restroom
facility.

I hate people in first class
who have no class.

I hate people who don't recycle.
I hate environmentalists who need a bath.

I hate grandparents who pinch cheeks.

I hate uncles who talk to you
like you're still a child.

I hate people who bring their
knitting with them.

I hate people who wear clothes that are too tight.

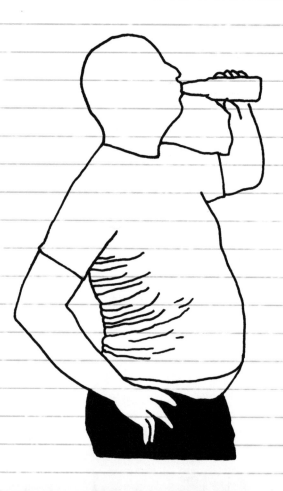

I hate certain people who wear clothes
that are too baggy.

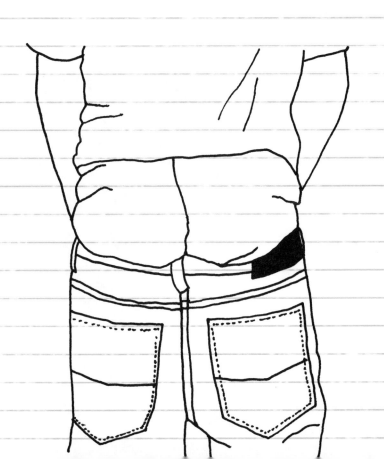

I hate blondes who ARE more fun.

I hate people who sit innocently
in shallow water, trying to hide
the fact that they are peeing.

I hate old men who wink.
I hate young men who wink.

I hate carefree people who
go everywhere barefoot.

I hate 99 percent of the people
who go to a nude beach.

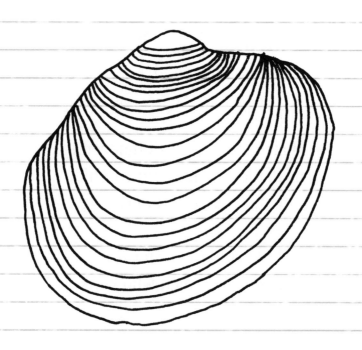

I hate plumbers and contractors who never call you back.
I hate plumbers who don't have the stereotypical butt crack showing.
I hate car salesmen who pounce on you like prey when you step onto their lot.
I hate mechanics who make up broken car part names to fix.

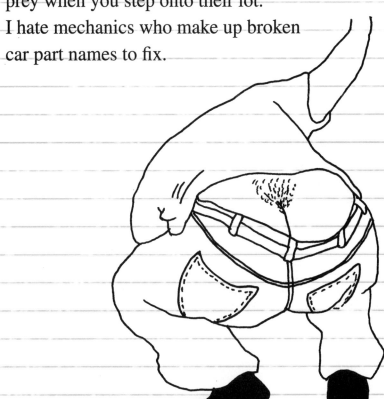

I hate anyone who still uses a phone book.

I hate cab drivers who take
the long route.
I hate high maintenance girls
who take forever to get ready.

I hate large morning radio
show casts.
I hate radio DJs with that fake
animated radio voice.
I hate idiots who speak loudly
because they are wearing
headphones.

I hate anyone who doesn't enjoy
jammin' wit Marley.

I hate people who save all the good seats at the movies.

I hate the movie theater armrest hogger.

I hate hogs who finish their popcorn before the movie starts.

I hate moviegoers who leave their trash in the theater.

I hate trashy people who ruin my movie experience.

I hate great actors who choose to be in dreadful movies.

I hate directors who remake classic pop culture flicks too soon.

I hate movie execs who decide to "reboot" failing franchises.

I hate Ferris's friend Cameron for destroying his father's beautiful antique Ferrari.
I hate people who spoil the end of movies for me.
I hate people who figure out the surprise twist at the beginning of the movie.

I hate people who are addicted to Angry Birds.
I hate people who have to have the
latest iPhone.
I hate people who are too connected.
I hate people who block their Wi-Fi.
I hate people who fear technology.

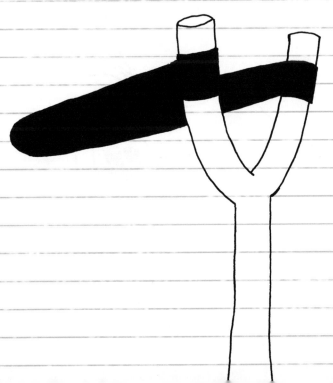

I hate people who are PCs who DON'T secretly want to be Macs.

I hate people who follow up with,
"I'm just sayin."

I hate everyone . . . I'm just sayin.

I hate people who have bad tattoos.

I hate people who pick their tattoo off of a parlor wall.

I hate people who have tattoos of more than one ex's name.

I hate people who have unfinished tattoos.

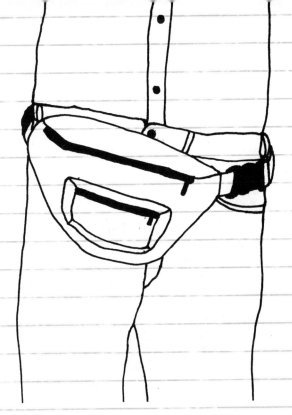

I hate all men who wear fanny packs.
I hate unfocused parachute packers.
I hate people who only pray when they
need something.

I hate the "spit talker."
I hate the "know-it-all."
I hate the "one-upper."

I hate barely pregnant women who rest their hands on top of their unnoticeable belly.
I hate people who want all the attention.
I hate people who wear maternity clothes who never had a baby.

I hate people who have dual citizenship.
I hate people who think they are better than me.
I hate people who are better than me.

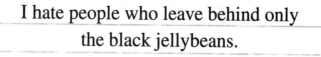

I hate people who leave behind only the black jellybeans.

I hate people who can swing dance.
I hate people who swing.

I hate people who knock something
before they try it.

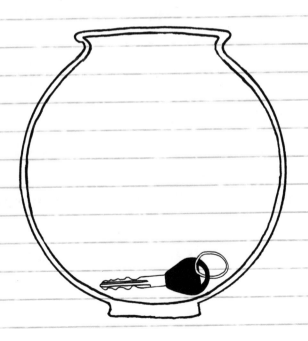

I hate people who can take their time and read
while doing their business.
I hate people who talk on the phone while in
the bathroom.
I hate guys who talk to you while at a urinal.

I hate guys who put their hand on the wall
above the urinal while peeing.
I hate guys who feel compelled to spit in
urinals before, after, and during the process . . .

I hate people who take the bathroom stall right next to you.

I HATE PEOPLE WHO DON'T COURTESY FLUSH.

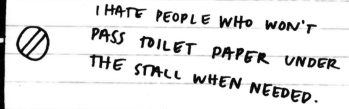

I HATE PEOPLE WHO WON'T PASS TOILET PAPER UNDER THE STALL WHEN NEEDED.

I hate people who take their drink into the bathroom.

I hate everyone who doesn't follow the unwritten public bathroom rules.

I hate club owners who make people work
for tips in public restrooms by handing out
paper towels.
I hate people who avoid washing their hands
so they don't have to tip the guy handing out
the paper towels.
I hate people who profit generously
from necessities.
I hate oil and banking
executives equally.

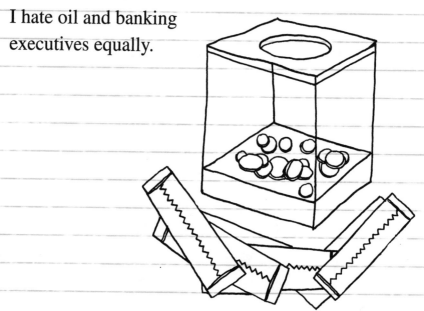

I hate people who come out
of a restroom laughing.

I hate comedians who have nothing
but potty humor.

I hate teachers for having the summer off.
I hate parents who think it's the teacher's job
to show their kids good manners.
I hate teachers who knew I didn't have the
answer and would call on me.
I hate teacher's pets.

I hate Hermione for not wanting Harry Potter.

I hate kids who have magic wands.

I hate bad magicians.

I hate anyone who didn't want to be a Goonie.

I hate depressed super heroes.

I hate Superman for not taking advantage of his X-ray vision.

I hate the Invisible Man for similar reasons.

I hate superheroes who don't have sidekicks.
I hate superheroes who keep their
identity secret.
I hate superheroes who don't have more clever
disguises than a pair of glasses.
I hate gullible people.
I hate people who won't poke fun at guys
in capes.

I hate vampires for not turning me into one of their kind.
I hate vampires who don't suck human blood.
I hate vampires who glisten in the sun.
I hate everyone who is now on the vampire bandwagon.

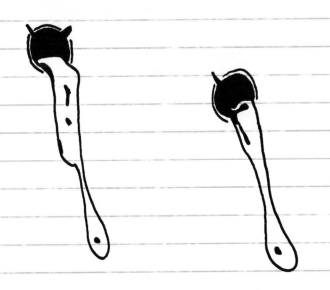

I hate people who are not on Team Jacob.

I hate all the Twihards who will write me hate mail over that one. (Actually, I kind of respect the hate mail.)

I hate girls whose milkshake doesn't bring all the boys to the yard.

I hate girls' hips that lie.

I hate the person who beat me
to bringing sexyback.

I absolutely hate whoever let the dogs out.

I hate anyone who doesn't know the
Time Warp Dance.

I hate anyone who doesn't know Pee-Wee's secret word of the day.

I hate Indiana Jones for not leaving well enough alone.

I hate people who didn't get lost watching *Lost*.
I hate the people who yell out the answers
while watching *Jeopardy!*
I hate anyone who doesn't know wrestling
is for real.
I hate people who don't sink their teeth into
shark week.
I hate people who go fishing, but are too
squeamish to take the fish off of the hook.

I hate the guy with the limp, dead-fish handshake.

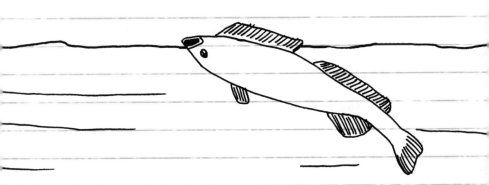

I hate Rocky's son for not becoming a boxer.

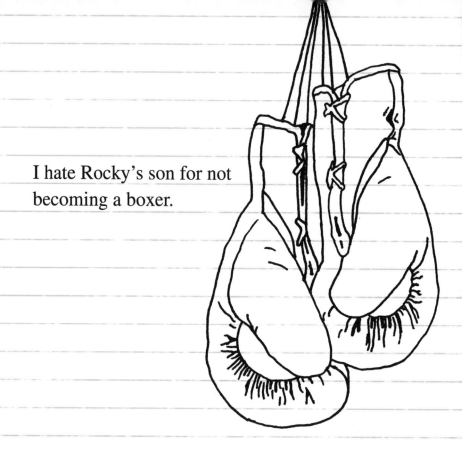

I hate Rocky for not naming his son something tougher, like Butch.

I hate anyone who still hasn't gotten milk?
I hate people who dunk things in milk.
I hate anyone can just drink cold milk any time
of day with any meal.
I hate creepy CGI babies in commercials.

I hate that I may be the only person who hates
Flo, the Progressive lady.
I hate anyone who hasn't Just Done It already.
I hate guys who still go around saying
"Wassssssssuuuuuupp?!"
I hate people who let them melt in their hands,
not their mouth.

I hate Spartans who have airbrushed abs.
I hate Ralphie for shooting his eye out.

I hate anyone who likes their martini stirred, not shaken.
I hate people who say their last name before their first.

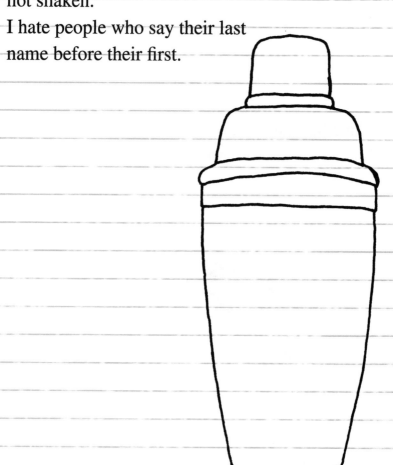

I hate people who add an S to words that aren't supposed to be plural.
I hate people who aren't yet on the Internets.
I hate people who use the words
"epic" and "fail."
I hate people who fail in epic ways.

I hate people who didn't take the
swine flu seriously. Oink.

I hate people who let their home
smell like their pets.

I hate dads who bring their young daughters into the men's room.

I hate people who get away with dating people half their age.

I hate show-offs.

I hate people who have too much and want
the world to see.

I hate people who have it and don't flaunt it.

I hate parents who are always right,
whether you believe them or not.

I hate people who will never admit when
they're wrong.

I hate people who know better. . . .

I hate people who only use their
dining room once a year.
I hate people who serve stale chips.
I hate people who skimp on food
when throwing a party.
I hate people who take back unopened
food that they brought to a party.
I hate people who don't serve
alcohol at their lame parties.

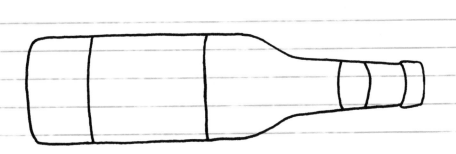

I hate people who don't need to drink to have a good time.

I hate people who exaggerate like a million times over.

I hate people who, um, use the word, um, in every other, um, breath.

I hate teenagers that like, use the word like, to describe, like, everything.

I hate people who don't like what I like.

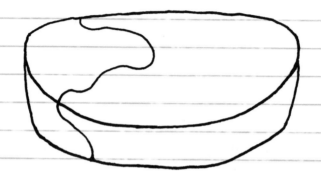

I hate people who use my bar of soap.

I hate people who leave an
unflushed toilet bowl behind.

I hate the person just before me
who warmed up the toilet seat.

I hate people who don't dust their house.
I hate lazy people who don't clean out the dryer
lint trap.
I hate people who leave the fridge door wide open.
I hate everyone who doesn't cover their food in
the microwave.
I hate people who put dishes in the sink . . .
which is right next to the dishwasher.
I hate people who fold laundry wrong.
I hate people who fill the dishwasher wrong.
I hate anyone who accuses me of doing
chores wrong.

I hate people who wonder why I don't do my share of the chores.

I hate people who don't realize I replace the empty toilet paper roll every time.

I hate my partner who asked to borrow my toothbrush.

I hate people who want to know why my ex and I broke up.

I hate nosy people.

I hate mailmen who know too much.
I hate "big brother" for always watching.
I hate people who call me "Bro" who have no
family relation.

I hate people who call me kiddo.
I hate people who call me honey, hon,
or sweetie.
I hate insanely jealous people.
I hate partners who won't tell me who just
texted them.

I hate people who give the silent treatment.
I hate people who won't tell me why they are
mad at me.
I hate people who assume I can read their mind.
I hate people who have been mad at someone
for so long, they can't remember why.

I hate people who hog the sheets.
I hate farmers who name their farm animals . . .
and then eat them.

I hate people who chew really loudly.
I hate slobs who talk with their mouth full.
I hate people who are done with a piece of gum
in three minutes.
I hate people who can chew the same piece
of gum for seven hours.

I hate people who make more than me, but do a LOT less.

I hate chatty people who leave long voicemail messages.

I hate people who "accidentally" open my mail.

I hate people who take their sweet ol' time.
I hate everyone who has the luxury of spare time.
I hate people who are too quick.

I hate people who are nervous.

I hate people with nerves of steel.

I hate anyone who uses kryptonite for evil plots.

I hate people who won't someday avenge me.

I hate dentists who ask me questions while
their hands are in my mouth.

I hate dentists for waiting so long to
finally make wearing braces look cool
with crazy colors.

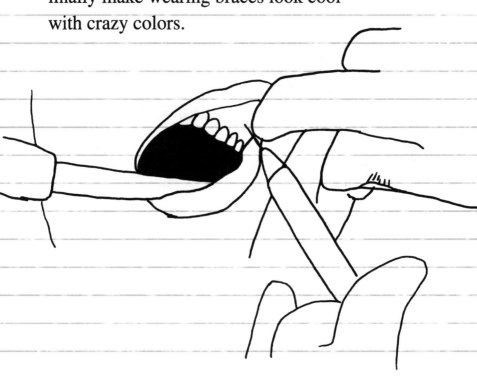

I hate doctors, especially during those "milestone" age checkups.
I hate doctors who charge me a co-pay to refer me to another doctor.

I hate doctors who I pay who tell me obvious things like, "I have to lose weight."

I hate stubborn people who refuse to go to a doctor.

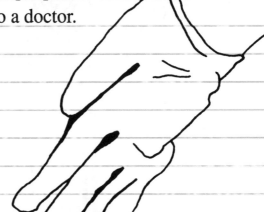

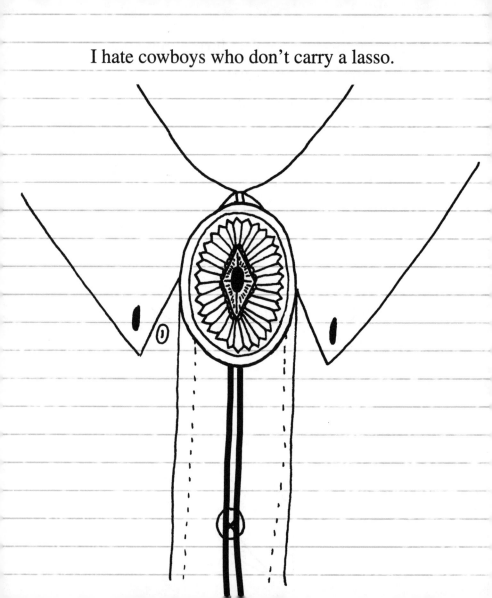

I hate Disney heroes who have
nothing distinguishable about them.

I hate massively muscle-bound action
stars who do Disney movies.

I hate anyone who constantly
cracks their knuckles.

I hate men who have always
had a beard, who shave it off.

I hate people who start by saying, "I don't mean to offend you . . . but," and then go ahead and do it anyway.

I hate people who can't hold their liquor.
I hate dates who order the most expensive thing on the menu.
I hate dates who don't at least pretend to offer to pay.
I hate dates who want to go "dutch."
I hate cheap dates.

I hate fortunetellers who never hit the lottery.

I hate kids with creepy voices in horror movies.

I hate people with fetishes.
I hate people who touch their feet.

I hate couples who lie on beds in furniture stores.

I hate kids who jump on freshly made beds.

I hate people who make their bed every day.

I hate people who have maids.

I hate neurotic people who clean before the cleaning service shows up.

I hate old people who should no longer
be driving.
I hate people who are old enough, but don't
get their driver's license.
I hate those people who DO get a license,
but shouldn't.
I hate timid drivers who drive sitting right
up against their steering wheel.
I hate punks who drive with their seat
lounged waaay back.

I hate jackasses who drive with their high beams on.
I hate tailgaters.
I hate people who can't keep up with me.
I hate people who drive someplace and have no recollection of anything along the way.

I hate backseat drivers.
I hate people who make me ride in the back
seat.
I hate people who ride in the back seat when
there are only two people in the car.
I think I hate everyone who drives while I'm on
the road.

I hate people who won't stop and ask for directions.

I hate people who finally stop and ask for directions and say: "Yeah, uh huh, okay, got it. Thanks!"

. . . Then walk away and ask the person they're with, "Did you get that?"

I hate people who are more concerned about everything around them than the road in front of them.

I hate ANYONE who tries to change my car's radio station.

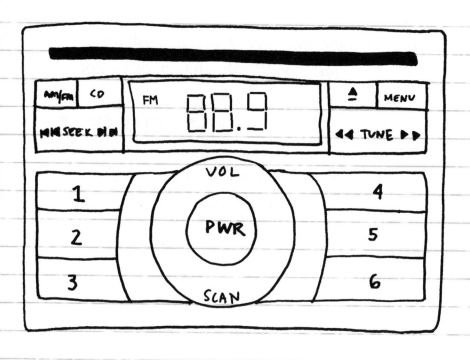

I hate people who park right next to my car in an empty parking lot.

I hate drivers who don't know how to change a flat tire.

I hate people who don't know how to pump their own gas.

I hate people who feel free to share their gas . . . in crowded elevators.

I hate lowlifes who cause accidents and blame it on the other person.

I hate people who don't take credit for what they do.

I hate people with bad credit who still shop for things they don't need.

I hate impulse shoppers.

I hate bank tellers who act like they have money.

AB-1234A
012344
AUTHORIZEDSIGNATURE
Notvalidunlesssigned
I HATE CASHIERS WHO DON'T CHECK MY CREDIT CARD SIGNATURE.
To Report a lost or stolen card, call toll-free 1800-555-1234.
VISA

YARD SALE

I hate thrifty people who shop at yard sales every weekend . . . then have yard sales of their own.

I hate savvy people who get a better deal than me.

I hate people who can stare me down.
I hate people who blink too much.
I hate people who hold things away from their
face in order to read them.

I hate jugglers who drop things.

I hate players.

I hate people who play games.

I hate people who are competitive about everything.

I hate kids who don't play outside.

I hate myself for sizing people up and down in the first two seconds I meet them.

I hate jewelers who size you up and down before they decide to help you.

I hate jewelers who bring out engagement rings in front of my girlfriend that are MUCH more than I can afford.

I hate men who propose in mundane ways.
I hate women who have to think about saying
yes to a proposal.

I hate men who give household items as gifts
to their wives.
I hate couples who just buy something for
themselves on holidays.
I hate couples who give gifts to their partner
of things that they wanted
for themselves.

I hate people who cut down trees.

I hate people who have fake Christmas trees . . .
but light a pine candle.

I hate adults with more than one stuffed animal.

I hate guys who sleep with stuffed animals.

I hate guys who rent chick flicks.

I hate girls who drag guys to chick flicks.

I hate guys who get emotional during
chick flicks.

I hate chick flick movie couples who have no
chemistry.

I hate chick flick movie couples who made the
movie while dating, but since have broken up.

I hate girls who hit.
I hate men who slap.

I hate football players who
smack each other's asses.

I hate people who say, "Go get 'em, tiger!"
I hate people who have animal instincts.
I hate couples who don't have animal attraction.

I hate people who complain, but have no idea what a bad day is.

I hate people who thrive on drama.

I hate people who are in the know.

I hate people who say no.

I hate people who hear what they want to hear.

I hate people who don't let their lovable dogs give them big sloppy kisses.

I hate poets who don't rhyme.

I hate chefs who aren't overweight.

I hate "artists" who create
simple abstract paintings.

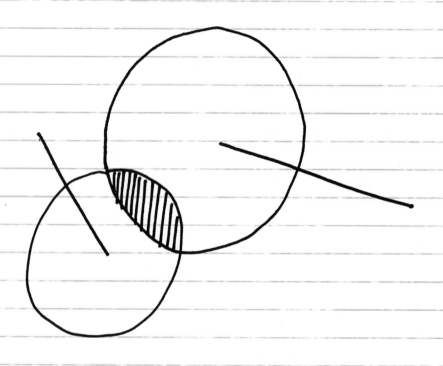

I hate non-talented graffiti artists.
I hate people who still wear airbrushed clothing.

I hate whoever wrote my phone number on the restroom wall.

I hate people who sing bad catchy tunes that get stuck in your head.

I hate people who still call for the person who owned my number before me.

I hate people who beat around the bush.

I hate phone solicitors who don't get to the point.

I hate good phone solicitors who win you over.

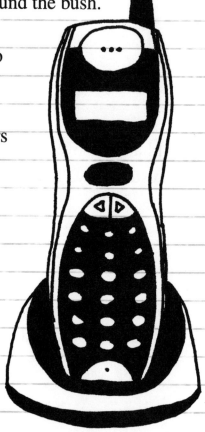

I hate guys who use pickup lines.

I hate girls who fall for pickup lines.

I hate guys who are full of hot air.

I hate girls who are full of it.

I hate people who don't make a grand entrance.

I hate people who don't have a theme song.

I hate people who come up with easy million-dollar ideas before I do . . . like the Snuggie.

I hate people who get all up in my business.

I hate musicians who sing songs about their exes.

I hate musically talented partners who didn't write songs about me.

I hate Oompa Loompas.

I hate people who wear fur coats.

I hate people who get mono more than once.

I hate people who have a midlife crisis early.
I hate people who don't know what they want
out of life.

I hate guys who only buy flowers to apologize.

I hate non-spontaneous people.

I hate people who don't like surprises.

I hate people who pretend they were surprised at their party.

I HATE PEOPLE WHO DON'T CELEBRATE THEIR BIRTHDAY.

I hate people who don't blow out all their birthday candles in one breath.

I hate other people who blow out MY birthday candles.

I hate people who tell everyone what they wished for.

I hate friends who tell me a secret, but I'm the last to know.
I hate friends who tell me secrets that they know I could never keep.

I hate people who make up new rules to the
game.
I hate people whose way is the only way.
I hate people who get in my way.
I hate people who don't try to get away with
breaking the rules.

I hate "vegans" . . . who make up their own
rules about what is vegan.
I hate vegetarians . . . who cheat and eat meat.

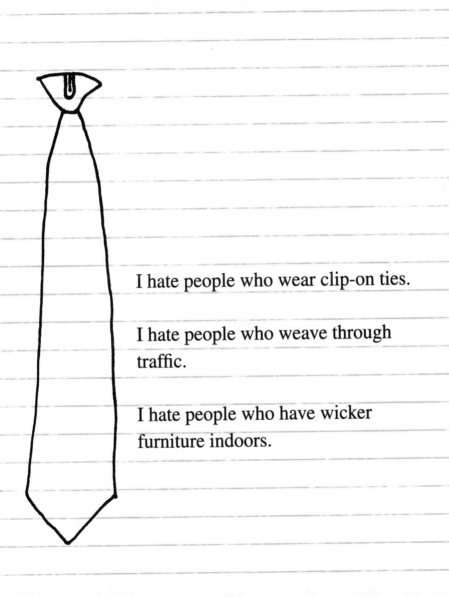

I hate people who wear clip-on ties.

I hate people who weave through traffic.

I hate people who have wicker furniture indoors.

I hate people who claim they only smoke when they drink.

I hate smokers who flick their cigarettes while driving.

I hate people who use bad cologne to try to hide the smoky clothes smell.

I hate smokers whose houses and cars smell like them.

I hate people who shake off their sandy towel upwind of me at the beach.

I hate kids who run by too close to your sand-free beach blanket.

I hate men who wear sandals . . . with dress socks.

I hate people who wear flowery tropical prints who aren't on vacation.

I hate coworkers who go away on lavish vacations and don't even bring back a small box of candy for the office.

I hate people who somehow can take multiple vacations a year.

I hate people who count down the days they have left while on vacation.

I hate people who count on me.

I hate the rich people who own those beautiful shore houses along the coast.

I hate fearless skyscraper construction workers who have their lunch up on a girder.

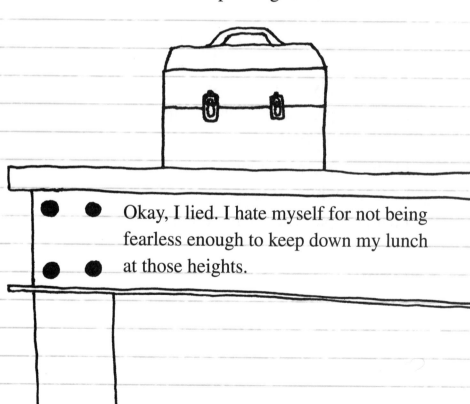

Okay, I lied. I hate myself for not being fearless enough to keep down my lunch at those heights.

I hate biker guys who don't have a big beer gut.

I hate people who CAN multitask while driving.

I hate people who know how to work the system.

I hate anyone who didn't let me cheat off of them in school.
I hate everyone who be smarter than I.
I hate anyone who is as smart as me.
I hate book smart people who have no street smarts.

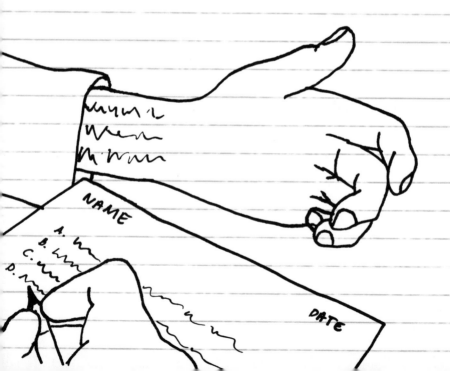

I hate intellectuals who use BIG words.

I hate people who make me feel small.

I hate people who think they are bigger than
they really are.

I hate the people who decide who's going to get laid off.

I hate brown-nosers.

I hate yes men.

I hate some people who look both ways before crossing the street.

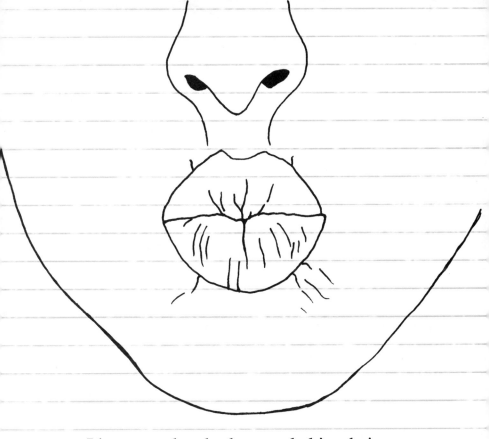

I hate people who let people kiss their ass.
I hate people who don't kiss back.
I hate people who kiss with their eyes open.

I hate pubescent guys who don't shave those seven long straggly chin hairs.

I hated everyone who reached puberty before me in gym class.

I hate boys who shave who don't have anything to shave yet.

I hate that one boy in high school who could grow a full Jesus beard.

I hate his parents for not making him shave.

I hate everyone whose yearbook picture
is better than mine.

I hate everyone who didn't sign my yearbook.

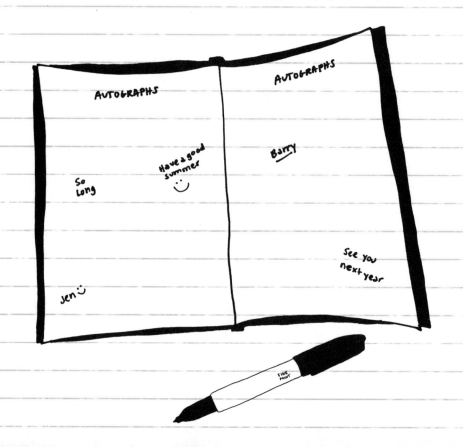

I hate people who thought they were the sh*t in high school.

I hate those people who peaked in high school.
I hate classmates who weren't nice to us nerds. . . .

I hate myself for poking fun at even nerdier nerds than me.

I hate people who have the last laugh.

I hate people who claim it's their birthday to try to get something free at a restaurant.

I hate people who sing "Happy Birthday" out of tune.
I hate people who know I gave them a re-gifted present.
I hate people who give thoughtless gift cards.

I hate people who I see re-gift something I gave them.

I hate people who forget my birthday . . .
especially in my own family.

I hate people who make me cut and serve my
own birthday cake.

I hate when people spell my name wrong in the card.

I hate people who underline the Hallmark words in my card . . . but write nothing personal.

I hate the person who eats the piece of cake with my name written in icing on it.

~~Jeniffer,~~
Jennifer,

Hope your
Birthday was
Great!!!!!!!

I hate parents who invite people who don't have kids to children's birthday parties.

I hate people who make up lame excuses why they can't come.

I hate people who are busted by social media after giving an excuse.

I hate people who only remember it's my birthday because Facebook reminded them.

I hate people who make me open gifts and
read my cards in front of everyone.
I hate family who send birthday cards
without money.
I hate people who only send me birthday
wishes via text.

I hate everyone who leaves my party right after
we serve the cake.

I hate people who send belated cards.
I hate people who don't bother to wish me
happy birthday.

I hate people who don't pick up their dog poop.
I hate people who noticed that my
dog pooped in their yard.
I hate people who are more noticeable than me.

I hate bartenders who look right past me and serve everyone around me.
I hate waiters who tell me they just ran out of the one thing I wanted on the menu.

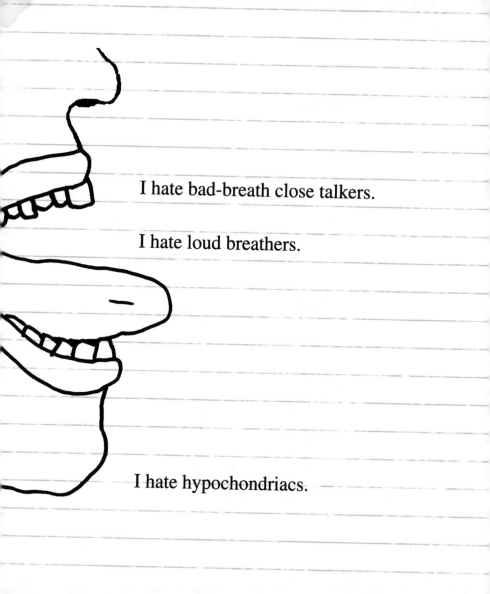

I hate bad-breath close talkers.

I hate loud breathers.

I hate hypochondriacs.

I hate people who . . . complete my sentence.

I hate the people who interrupt my five-minute lunch break with, "I don't want to bother you during lunch."

I hate people who have time to complain about how "busy" they are at work, but who I watch leave on time every day.

I hate coworkers who never work late, who make a comment the one day I leave five minutes early.

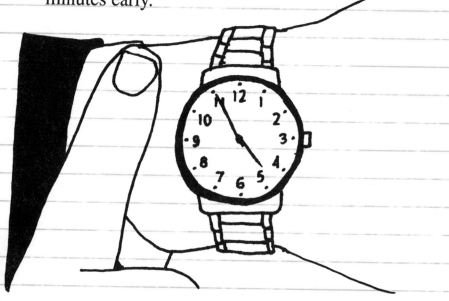

I hate people who talk too much.

I hate car salesmen who just don't give me a fair price without haggling.

I hate the drunk touchy-feely guy.

I hate the smoker who doesn't tap off the cigarette ashes.

I hate powerful people who don't do good with their power.

I hate people who don't realize the machines
are slowly taking over our world.
I hate dictators who do the same.
I hate Nostradamus and his prophecies.
I hate people who actually think the world will
end during their lifetime.

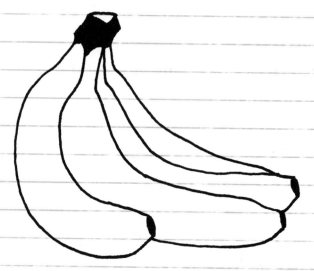

I hate people who actually prepared an emergency food and water stash at the turn of the millennium.

I hate the apes who will rise to power on our planet.

I hate the person who hits the slot machine
jackpot right next to me.
I hate people who always win.
I hate anyone who has ever hit the lottery.
I hate people who actually think they're going
to win the lottery.

I hate people who believe everything they read on the Internet.

I hate people who think they are dying because they went online to diagnose themselves.

I hate people who give up too easily.

I hate people who don't do the Thriller dance whenever it's played at a party.

I hate people who have a single karaoke
song that is theirs and only theirs to sing every
time they go out.

I hate people who think they have talent.

I hate bad cover bands.

I hate people who play Rock Band video games and think they are real musicians.

I hate people who don't chase their dreams.

I hate people who are afraid they will fail.

I hate people who succeed before me.

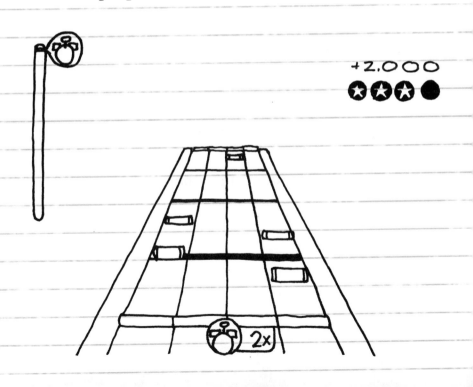

I hate people who make me go in front of them on an escalator.

I hate people who stand too close to me in an elevator.

I hate people who have a fear of bridges.

I hate people who don't face their fears.

I hate people who try to scare me during an
intense movie scene.
I hate the someone rapping, rapping, rapping at
my chamber door.

I hate the sex-crazed, pot-smoking counselors who let Jason Voorhees drown on Friday the 13th.

I hate people who let their nails grow too long.

I hate Peter Benchley for writing *Jaws* and making me forever fear all open water.

I hate people who are afraid of everything.

I hate people who don't try new things.

I hate people who don't dream big.

I hate people who don't encourage you to try.

I hate people who want to see you fail.

I hate people who miss the point of this book.

I hate people who talk behind your back.

I hate people who catch me talking behind
their back.

I hate people who can actually play golf well.
I hate people who seriously think
golf is a real sport.
I hate people who say bowling isn't.
I hate everyone's negative energy.

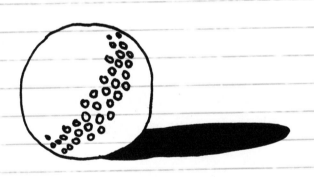

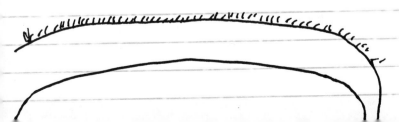

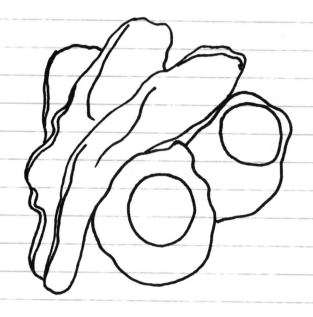

I hate people who go out for breakfast and
only order fruit and yogurt.

I hate people who order the healthy option
then take a piece of my bacon.

I hate people who call me while eating breakfast and cause my cereal to go soggy.

I hate people who waste food.

I hate people who will eat long-overripe, soft, squishy fruit.

I hate everyone who has a good sexy story that starts with, "One time, at band camp . . . ."

I hate people who let their food rot in the office fridge.

I hate people who actually eat food that isn't theirs out of the work fridge.

I hate the people who leave their dirty dishes in the office sink.

I hate whoever took my stapler.

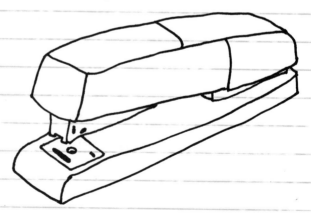

I hate coworkers who book meetings at noon.

I hate coworkers who make me buy the crap their kid is selling.

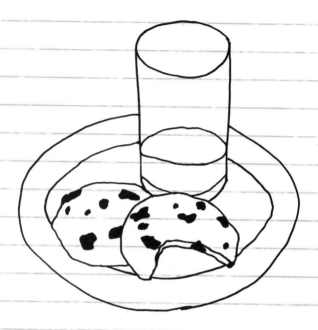

I hate my parents for leading me to believe that
Santa was real . . . until I was thirteen.

I hate the kids in school who told me Santa
wasn't real.

I hate people who spread stories about me.

I hate people I have to confront.

I hate people who confront me.

I hate adults who never grew up.

I hate kids who act like grownups.

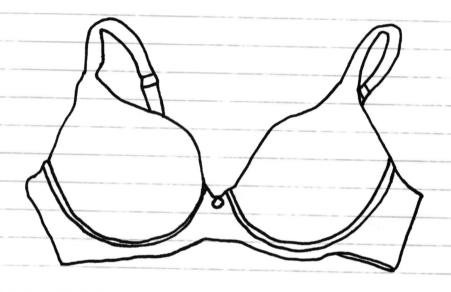

I hate people who don't want a bachelor party.
I hate friends who throw lame bachelor parties.
I hate anyone who believes that women aren't
naughtier than men.

I hate people who don't let it "stay in Vegas."
I hate boring people who play it safe.
I hate people who are okay with soaking in
hotel tubs.
I hate the person who makes the wake up call to
my hotel room.

I hate brothers and sisters who aren't close.
I hate family who make it difficult to be close.
I hate twins who don't dress identically.
I hate twins who don't take advantage of being
a twin.

I hate people who get angry with you when you try and do something nice for them.

I hate everyone who has done body shots off of my significant other.
I hate unappreciative people.

I hate people who won't admit that they've rocked out to Bon Jovi . . . and LOVED it.

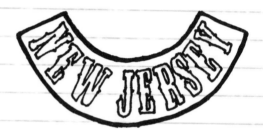

I hate whoever gave love a bad name.

I hate bands with lousy names.

I hate lead singers who go out on their own without their band.

I hate bands who actually try to replace a lead singer.

I hate born leaders.

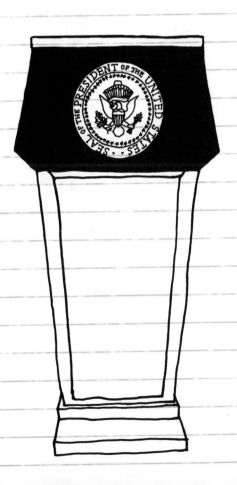

I hate people who say the music when they were growing up was better.

I hate us for finally being right.

I hate anyone who doesn't like '80s music.
I hate anyone who still wears '80s fashions.
I hate people who wear skin tight,
flesh-colored pants.

I hate people who ask me, "does this make me look fat?"

I hate people who get angry with me for being honest.

I hate kids for their unfiltered honesty.
I hate anyone who thinks overalls make them look sexy.

I hate people who fake singing our national anthem because they don't know the words.

I hate people who overcook my eggs.

I hate people who complain about my cooking, but don't cook.

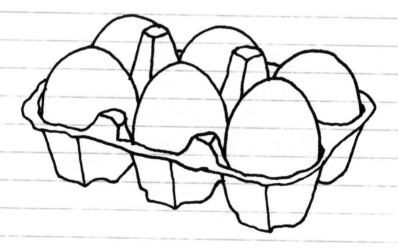

I hate anyone who can drink me under the table.

I hate bartenders who ask for everyone's ID . . . but mine.

I hate people who know what's in the secret sauce.

I hate anyone who knows the ancient Chinese secret.

I hate everyone who doesn't know how many licks it takes to get to the center of a Tootsie Pop.

I hate talented people who can watch two TV shows at once by flipping back and forth.

I hate the 8:00 TV news anchor who teases me with the 10:00 weather forecast.

I hate weather forecasters who still have a job the next day after they are SO wrong.

I hate people who go crazy and buy up all the bread and milk at the first report of snow.

I hate anyone who isn't counting down until McDonald's Shamrock Shakes are back again.

I hate people who address people as ma'am or mister.

I hate people who use indoor couches, outside.

I hate people who have done the things on MY bucket list.

I hate family members who make us gather for dinner at the early bird hour.

I hate people who can't stray from their routine.
I hate people who need a routine.

I hate reality TV stars who think they
are celebrities.
I hate people who expect something
for nothing.
I hate people who don't just abandon the
futile combover.

I hate people who invent things that I thought of first.
I hate friends who get angry that you don't keep in touch . . . but they don't either.
I hate people who read assembly instruction manuals.

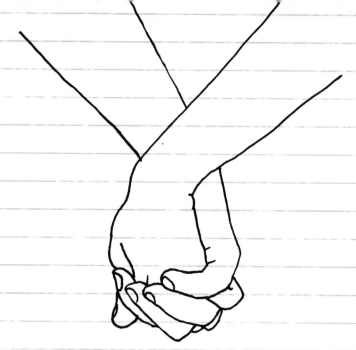

I hate people who thrive on office gossip.
I hate coworkers who date.
I hate secret lovers who think we
don't know about them.
I hate anyone who has set me up
on a blind date.

I hate people who have a different voice when talking to their significant other.

I hate people I haven't seen in a long time who ask, "So, what's new?" . . . and I have nothing good to tell them.

I hate the professional corporate me.

I hate people who always look angry.

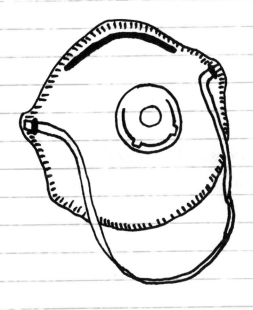

I hate people who have exhaled out the same air
I'm breathing in.

I hate everyone who doesn't like pizza.
I hate anyone else who doesn't want any
toppings on their pizza.

I hate people who fold their slice of pizza
in half to eat it.
I hate people who start with the crust.
I hate people who live on the wild side.

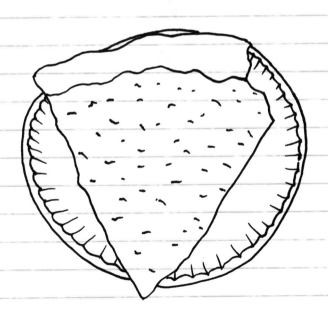

I hate people who think the grass is always greener on the other side.

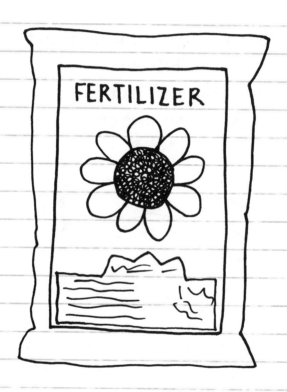

I hate everyone who finds out it is.

I hate people who take the road less traveled.
I hate anyone who takes the long way home.
I hate everyone who takes the easy way out.

I hate spies who know how to go "dark."
I hate the CIA for not stealing me as an infant
and turning me into a Super Spy.
I hate people who have more than one identity.
I hate people who have no personality.

I hate several of my multiple personalities.

RIGHT BACK AT YOU!

I hate egomaniacs.

I hate people who have alter egos who I like more than them.

I hate people who put up with people's crap.

I hate people who think their sh*t doesn't stink.

I hate people who can't put up with my sh*t.

I hate people who feel like it's their duty to fix me.

I hate immature people who chuckle
whenever someone says "duty."

(I hate that I'm one of those people.)

I hate people who laugh at their own jokes.
I hate people who laugh at everything.

I hate people who have annoying laughs.

I hate people who don't have a sense of humor.

I hate people who don't have MY sense
of humor.

I hate people who read most of this book in the
store, but don't buy it.

I hate people who are afraid to buy this book
for what people might think.

I hate EVERYONE who can't take a joke.

I hate people who only have one thing on their mind.

I hate people who hate this book.

I hate anyone who hates as much as me.

I hate everyone who thinks I meant to offend them personally.

I especially hate that one English teacher who told me I'd never be a writer. (You know who you are.)

I hate people who single people out.
I hate people who underestimate me.

I hate people who will be mad at me when they realize they are in this book.

I hate that people will ask if they are in the book.

I hate the people who don't realize they're in this book.

I hate people who don't understand the definition of **everyone**.

I hate people who need extra attention:

ev·ery·one (pronoun)

ev·ery·one [évvree wùn] or ev·ery·bod·y [évvree bòddee]

every person, whether of a defined group or in general

I hate everyone who still doesn't get it.

I hate lovers.

I hate haters of haters.

I hate people.

I hate everyone!!!

I hate people who overuse exclamation points!!!

You know whom I can stand maybe just a little tiny bit?

NO ONE. Because I hate everyone.

(I hate you, if you saw that coming.)

I hate myself for personally being some of "those" people in my book more often than I'd like to admit.

I hate that probably everyone has earned a place in this book at one time or another.

I hate myself if I've missed anyone.
I hate forgetful people.
I hate people who need instructions . . .

_____
_____
_____
_____
_____
_____
_____

I hate that we probably have so much in common.
I'd hate it if you made it into my next book.

So Many More People to Hate!

Social media is full of irritating people we can't stand. So follow along with posts from your fellow haters and reply back about "those" people you hate too!

Facebook: I Hate Everyone
Twitter: @EveryoneIHate
www.TheHatePage.com

And, since there may be a lot of things you hate too. . . .

I Hate Everything. is in stores and online everywhere along with the *I Hate Everything.* calendar and *I Hate Everything.: The Journal You Hate to Write In.*

Facebook: I Hate Everything
Twitter: @WhatIHateToday

Acknowledgments . . .

I hate people who leave before the credits role.

Though the title of this book might suggest otherwise, believe it or not, there really are a few good people out there who deserve acknowledgment . . . and I can't hate, including:

My publisher, Adams Media for bringing such an awesome book to the world.

My editor, Brendan O'Neill for skillfully making hating so much fun.

Lis and Adri for showing off their artistic and promotional talents for everyone.

My Super-Agent, Taryn Fagerness, for using her tremendous super powers to bring the hate to life.

And my girlfriend Jen, my Mom and Dad, my brother and sister, Klara, and all my friends and coworkers who tolerate all of my open loathing . . . and who look the other way when they "think" there may be an entry about them.

I hate that my dog may be the only one who understands me.

I hate that my dog loves EVERYONE back, no matter what.

I hate that one of us has a lot to learn.